The Slave Boy of Pompeii

Bernard Smith

Easystart

Series Editors: Andy Hopkins and Jocelyn Potter

1.1 What's the book about?

Look at the pictures on the front of the book and on page 1.

1 Talk about the pictures. What can you see?

2 What do you know about Pompeii? Why is it a famous town?

3 Tick (✓) the right answers. What do you think?

a What country is Pompeii in?

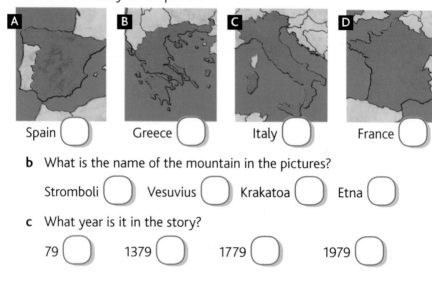

Spain ◯   Greece ◯   Italy ◯   France ◯

b What is the name of the mountain in the pictures?

Stromboli ◯   Vesuvius ◯   Krakatoa ◯   Etna ◯

c What year is it in the story?

79 ◯   1379 ◯   1779 ◯   1979 ◯

1.2 What happens first?

Look at the pictures on pages 1–3. Are the sentences right (✓) or wrong (✗)?

1 ◯ It is winter in Pompeii.

2 ◯ The boy lives in a big, expensive house.

3 ◯ The boy and the animal are friends.

4 ◯ Some people are unhappy about the mountain.

It is one o'clock on a hot summer day in August. In this old Roman town under the **mountain**, people are eating and drinking in their houses. There are people in the streets and in the shops. They are happy. They don't know. But we know.

The year is 79. The name of the mountain behind the town is Vesuvius. And Vesuvius is a **volcano**.

mountain /ˈmaʊntən/ (n) Go up the *mountain* and you can see the sea.
volcano /vɒlˈkeɪnəʊ/ (n) Etna is a famous *volcano* in Sicily.

1

Marcus Sextus is an important man in Pompeii. He and his family live in a big white house with a beautiful long garden.

Marcus Sextus and his family have fifteen **slaves**. There are eight men and six women, and there is one slave boy. His name is Mico. He works in the kitchen and the garden. Marcus Sextus is good to his slaves. They work all day and they have no money. But they have good food and they sleep in the house.

Young Mico has only one good friend. It is Fortunatus, the house **dog**. He is a big animal, black and strong.

slave /sleɪv/ (n) A *slave* works for no money.
dog /dɒg/ (n) I take my *dog* for a walk every day.

Usually Fortunatus stays in the small room behind the door. He sits there on a **chain** every day and watches the street. Bad people never come into the house. They are **afraid** of Fortunatus.

Today some friends of Marcus Sextus are visiting him in his house. The mountain is making **loud** noises and they are afraid.

'The **gods** of the mountain are angry,' a man says.

chain /tʃeɪn/ (n) We can't drive there. There's a *chain* across the road.
afraid /əˈfreɪd/ (adj) Small animals are *afraid* of big animals.
loud /laʊd/ (adj) I can't hear you. The television is very *loud*.
　　　　　　　　Please be quiet. You're talking very *loudly*.
god /gɒd/ (n) Jupiter and Mars are names of old Roman *gods*.

'The mountain often makes noises,' Marcus Sextus says to his friend. 'Every year we hear noises from it and sometimes **smoke** comes from it. But the gods are not angry. It isn't **dangerous**.'

Suddenly they hear a noise behind them. It is Fortunatus. He is dancing on his chain and making a loud noise.

'Be quiet, Fortunatus!' Marcus Sextus says.

But the dog doesn't stop.

'Bring the boy Mico here,' Marcus Sextus says to a slave. 'We can't talk with that noise. The boy can take the dog into the garden.'

smoke /sməʊk/ (n) Is there a problem in the kitchen? I can see *smoke*.
dangerous /ˈdeɪndʒərəs/ (adj) We can't swim in the sea here. It's *dangerous*.

The slave gets Mico and brings him to the door to the street.

'Marcus Sextus and his friends are talking about important things,' he says. 'And the dog is making a **terrible** noise. Take him into the garden and stay with him.'

The slave takes Fortunatus's chain in his hand. But suddenly the dog runs into the street.

The slave is very angry. 'Go after him quickly,' he says to Mico. 'Catch him and bring him back here.'

terrible /ˈterəbəl/ (adj) It's a *terrible* day today. It's cold and it's raining.

2.1 Were you right?

Look at your answers to Activity 1.2 on page ii. Then finish the sentences.

1 In Pompeii it is the month of ....

2 Marcus Sextus has a big house with a beautiful ....

3 Marcus Sextus and his family have fifteen ....

4 Mico's one friend is Fortunatus, the house ....

5 The mountain often makes a loud ....

6 The name of the mountain is ....

2.2 What more did you learn?

Finish the sentences with words from the boxes.

1 Marcus Sextus's house is .... and ....

| small | long | beautiful | big |

2 Fortunatus is a .... , ... dog.

| big | fat | little | strong |

3 Mico usually works in the .... and the ....

| garden | street | bedroom | kitchen |

4 On page 2 Fortunatus is .... and ....

| angry | happy | friendly | sleeping |

5 On page 3 Fortunatus is ....

| afraid | friendly | sleeping | watching |

6 Smoke .... comes from the mountain.

| never | always | sometimes | usually |

2.3 Language in use

**Look at the sentence on the right.
Then look at the pictures. Put the
words from the box into the sentences.**

> Usually Fortunatus stays **in** the
> small room **behind** the door.

under   from   in front of   in   behind   with

1 Mico and Fortunatus are .... a tree .... the
   garden.

2 They are playing .... a ball.

3 The slaves bring the food .... the kitchen.

4 An old slave is standing .... Marcus Sextus.

5 There is a drink on the table .... him.

2.4 What happens next?

What do you think? Write Yes or No.

1 Mico brings Fortunatus back to the house.   ....

2 Mico can't find Fortunatus.   ....

3 Marcus Sextus is angry with Mico.   ....

4 The noise from the mountain stops.   ....

5 Mico and Fortunatus run from the town into the country. ....

M ico runs into the street and looks for Fortunatus. The
dog is waiting for Mico near the house. Mico walks
across the street slowly and quietly and takes the chain in his
hand. The dog is quiet now but he is **shaking**. He is very
afraid.

Suddenly Mico hears a terrible loud noise behind him. He
looks back. A big **cloud** of heavy black smoke is coming from
the mountain behind the town. The street is shaking under
his feet.

Then Fortunatus runs away again. This time he takes
Mico with him. In a short time the town is behind them and
they are in the country.

shake /ʃeɪk/ (v) The old man's hands are *shaking*.
cloud /klaʊd/ (n) Dark *clouds* bring rain.

8

A long time later Mico and Fortunatus are under some small trees. It is late in the evening now. The **sky** is dark with black smoke. They can see the town of Pompeii behind a small **hill**. Clouds of smoke and **fire** are coming from the mountain. Big red hot **stones** and fire are falling on the houses in the town. There are fires in some houses. The dog is shaking.

'Let's stay here,' Mico says to the dog. 'We can sleep here. In the morning perhaps we can go back to the house.'

sky /skaɪ/ (n) We can see the sun in the *sky*.
hill /hɪl/ (n) A *hill* is a small mountain.
fire /faɪə/ (n) Are you cold? Sit near the *fire*.
stone /stəʊn/ (n) There are some big *stones* in my garden. I can't move them.

It is late in the night now. Suddenly small, hot stones fall from the dark sky. They fall on the trees and on the **ground**. Some stones fall on Mico and Fortunatus too. The small stones aren't heavy. They are very light. But there are some heavy stones too and they are very hot. They fall on the ground and smoke comes from them. Some stones hit Mico and Fortunatus.

'This is dangerous,' Mico says. He and Fortunatus go under a big tree and stay there. Fortunatus is very unhappy and afraid.

ground /graʊnd/ (n) Put that down on the *ground*. It's very heavy.

10

Now Mico and Fortunatus are sleeping under the tree. After a short time the stones stop, but then **ash** falls. The ash is light and it stays on the ground.

In the early morning Mico and Fortunatus look at the trees and the hills. The sky is dark with the smoke from the volcano. No ash is falling now, but there is a white coat of ash on the ground and on every tree. Fortunatus and Mico are white too.

ash /æʃ/ (n) The fire is dead now; there is only *ash* on the ground.

Suddenly there is a terrible noise again from the mountain and the ground shakes under them. A river of fire is running down the mountain. Fortunatus is afraid and runs away again. The dog is big and strong and Mico can't stop him.

After a long time Fortunatus finds a quiet place under some fruit trees and stops. Mico sits on the ground with him and talks to him quietly.

'Be a good dog, Fortunatus,' he says. 'We're OK here. Perhaps we can find a house and some people.'

Suddenly Fortunatus's head comes up. He can hear people near them. Now Mico can hear them too. They see four men under the trees. The men have big **sticks** in their hands.

'Look, Fortunatus,' he says. 'Some men. We're OK now.'

The four men are slaves and they work in the country. They stand quietly and look at Mico and the dog.

stick /stɪk/ (n) I can only walk with a *stick*.

3.1 Were you right?

1 Look at your answers to Activity 2.4. Are they right or wrong?

2 Circle the right words in the sentences.

a Fortunatus is *never / sometimes* afraid.

b The dog *wants / doesn't want* the boy with him.

c Mico *can / can't* take the dog home now.

d Fortunatus takes Mico *into / away from* Pompeii.

e The boy and the dog run into the *hills / town*.

f *Heavy / Light* stones fall on them from the sky first.

g The boy and the dog *can / can't* sleep in the night.

h They see fire on the mountain in the *night / morning*.

i *Black / White* ash falls on them.

j In the morning the sky is *blue / dark*.

k Fortunatus runs away again in the *night / morning*.

l Mico sees four men and he is *happy / unhappy*.

3.2 What more did you learn?

What comes first? And then? Write the numbers 1–8.

A ◯ Ash falls from the sky.

B ◯ Light stones fall on them from the sky.

C ◯ A river of fire runs down the mountain.

D ◯ They see four men in the trees.

E ◯ Mico finds Fortunatus in the street.

F ◯ They sleep under a tree.

G ◯ A big cloud of smoke comes from the mountain.

H ◯ Fortunatus takes Mico into the country.

3.3 Language in use

Look at the sentences on the right. Then write answers to the questions.

> The small stones aren't **heavy**.
> They're very **light**.

1 Are the small stones heavy?

   No, they aren't. They're light.

2 Is the coffee cold?

   ....

3 Is the car old?

   ....

4 Are the windows closed

   ....

5 Is Mico tall?

   ....

6 Is Fortunatus small?

   ....

7 Is Marcus Sextus thin?

   ....

8 Is the sky at night light?

   ....

3.4 What happens next?

What do you think? Write Yes or No.

1 The four men are friendly and take Mico to a house.   ....

2 The four men are afraid and run away from them.   ....

3 The four men hit Mico with their sticks.   ....

4 Mico and Fortunatus find Marcus Sextus and his family again.   ....

'Who are you?' one of the men asks.
'My name is Mico,' Mico says. 'And this is Fortunatus, my dog.'

'They're from Pompeii. I know it,' a man says. His face is white and he is afraid. He shakes his stick at Mico. 'The gods are angry with the people of Pompeii. They are bad people,' he says. 'The fire from the mountain is falling on that town and the people there are all dead. Go away, boy. We don't want the fire here.' And he hits Mico with his stick.

Fortunatus makes an angry noise and stands in front of Mico. The men hit Mico and the dog with their sticks. One man hits Mico on the head and he falls to the ground.

'Stop! Stop! What are you doing?'

The four men stop and look behind them. A tall Roman man is standing there with one of his house slaves.

The four men stand quietly. They are afraid of this man.

'Who are you, boy?' the tall man asks loudly.

'I'm Mico, a slave from the house of Marcus Sextus in Pompeii,' Mico says quietly.

'Marcus Sextus?' the man says. 'He's my brother. And this dog? Is his name Fortunatus?'

Fortunatus hears his name. He makes a quiet, friendly noise and puts his head on the man's foot.

'Fortunatus,' the man says again. He smiles and puts his hand on the dog's head. 'We know him well here. His father is my old dog, Rex.'

He looks at the four slaves with sticks. 'Go away!' he says and they run away quickly.

'Take this boy and the dog to our house,' he says to his house
slave. 'Wash them and find food and drink for them. Be very good to
them. I don't understand it, but the gods are their friends.'

Mico and Fortunatus go with the slave to a big house behind the
trees. The tall man looks at the red sky and the fire from the volcano.

'Fortunatus,' he says. 'A clever dog perhaps. He is afraid and runs
to his old house with his young friend. But the people in Pompeii,
my brother and his family ... they are all dead. And who lives? Only a
dog and a slave boy. Who can understand the games of the gods?'

Talk about it

Work with a friend. You live in Pompeii. The mountain is making loud noises and the houses are shaking. Do you stay in the town or do you go away? Talk about it.

| Student A | You are Marcus Sextus. You are not afraid of the mountain. Why not? |

| Student B | You are Marcus Sextus's friend. You are afraid. Why? What can you do? Where can you go? How? |

Write about it

A young man in Misenum, a town across the sea from Pompeii, sees the smoke and fire from Vesuvius. His name is Pliny and he is now a famous man. Finish his story.

24th ¹............................. Year 79

In the early afternoon my mother sees a big white cloud of
²......................... in the sky. It is coming from the ³........................,
Vesuvius. It is across the ⁴......................... from here and near the
⁵......................... of Pompeii. My family and I go into our garden and
⁶......................... at the big cloud in the sky. Then suddenly small,
light stones fall on us.

Later in the night fire ⁷......................... down the mountain. In the
morning we can't ⁸......................... the houses in the towns near the
mountain. There is only stones and ash. The ⁹......................... in the
towns are all dead.

1. There are many old Roman towns in Europe and North Africa. In the big, expensive houses there are often pictures in the floors. Little stones of many colours make the mosaic pictures. Some mosaics are small. Some are very big. Talk about this mosaic of a house dog from a floor in a house in Pompeii. Perhaps it is Fortunatus. How do people make pictures with little stones?

2 **Work with three or four friends. Two or three of you are Romans and you live in a big, expensive house. One of you is a slave. You make mosaic pictures for the house.**

a The Romans want a new mosaic in the floor of their house. What do you want in your picture? A man, a woman, a god, an animal? Send the slave away and talk about it.

b Now the Romans describe the picture to the slave. The slave draws the picture in black and white.

c The Romans look at the picture. Is it good? Is it the right picture? Can the slave draw well?

d The Romans are happy with the picture. The slave can now draw the little stones on the picture with a black pen.

e The Romans describe the colours to the slave. Then he can colour the stones.

3 **Put up your pictures in a room. Now people can come and see them. First make a poster for your pictures. On the poster answer the questions:**

What are your pictures?

Where can people see them?

When can people see them?